YOUR KNOWLEDGE HAS

Markus Rothenhöfer

Development of a Location Validation Web Service

In the context of the Web Technologies Seminar

GRIN Verlag

Bibliografische Information der Deutschen Nationalbibliothek:

Die Deutsche Bibliothek verzeichnet diese Publikation in der Deutschen National-
bibliografie; detaillierte bibliografische Daten sind im Internet über http://dnb.d-
nb.de/ abrufbar.

Imprint:

Copyright © 2012 GRIN Verlag GmbH
Druck und Bindung: Books on Demand GmbH, Norderstedt Germany
ISBN: 978-3-656-24999-3

This book at GRIN:

http://www.grin.com/en/e-book/198397/development-of-a-location-validation-web-
service

GRIN - Your knowledge has value

Der GRIN Verlag publiziert seit 1998 wissenschaftliche Arbeiten von Studenten, Hochschullehrern und anderen Akademikern als eBook und gedrucktes Buch. Die Verlagswebsite www.grin.com ist die ideale Plattform zur Veröffentlichung von Hausarbeiten, Abschlussarbeiten, wissenschaftlichen Aufsätzen, Dissertationen und Fachbüchern.

Visit us on the internet:

http://www.grin.com/

http://www.facebook.com/grincom

http://www.twitter.com/grin_com

Development of a

Location Validation Web Service

Term Paper
In the context of the Web Technologies Seminar

Department of Information Systems

Author: Markus Rothenhöfer

Submit date: 2012-05-24

Table of Contents

1   Introduction

In many applications unverified data is processed, which often leads to inconsistence or errors. Therefore the need for applications to validate this data is high. A lot of types of data can be verified easily but more complex user data such as full-text-addresses pose a great challenge towards validation.

This paper proposes an exemplary solution for such a validation by describing the development of a web service that allows a research conference database[1] to validate conference-location-strings. The validation consists of checking the plausibility of the location string, correction and standardization of the spelling, classification (City, State, Country, etc.) and providing corresponding data such as latitude and longitude. For this purpose, the web service accesses the GeoNames database. Consequently, the conference database receives a rich response which it can also use to provide further information, e.g., embedded maps or HTML5-Microdata-Markup.

The remainder of the paper is outlined as follows. In Section 2 the basic technologies for the realization of the project are introduced. A special focus is given to the understanding of web services and the current implementation approaches. In Section 3 the actual problem is broken down into technical requirements and technical conception. Afterwards, in Section 4 the implementation will be explained. In Section 5, by using sample data the sufficient reliability towards validation accuracy is tested. Finally, in Section 6 a conclusion is drawn and further research opportunities are outlined.

---

[1] The conference database can be access here: http://dbis-group.uni-muenster.de/conferences/

2 Basics

For the realization in the following Sections a basic understanding of major technologies is necessary. First, an overview over the current web service implementation styles is given and a concrete PHP-framework for the implementation is introduced. Afterwards the GeoNames database is presented.

2.1 Web Services

According to the [FGA+04] and [Alo04 p.124 - 125] web services consist of loosely connected software components which communicate with each other over a wide area network such as the internet. Furthermore, as stated in [LLS06] they are not bound to one operating system or programming language.

> "A Web service is a software system designed to support interoperable machine-to-machine interaction over a network", W3C-Consortium [1]

Two main approaches for the implementation of web services can currently be observed in the internet. On the one hand, there is the SOAP/WSDL approach. These technologies have mainly been established by Microsoft and IBM. On the other hand, in the last years also 'RESTful' web services have gained great popularity – especially in the context of Web 2.0 - and seem to have overtaken SOAP.

In the following both of these implementation styles will be introduced briefly.

2.1.1 SOAP/WSDL

Simple Object Access Protocol (SOAP) was the first broadly accepted web service type and is well documented [2]. It has been released in 1999 and became especially popular in the enterprise context. By using SOAP one can serialize methods and their environment and make them available to clients.

Due to the fact that SOAP works on an abstract layer it can be used independently towards protocols and transportation layers [GCD05 p. 792]. This means whilst working on the web service the developer is not affected by the protocol. Furthermore, later it is effortless possible to change the protocol. In contrast to these advantages, as stated in [PZL08], a SOAP-implementation might create overhead because each abstraction layer increases complexity and traffic.

According to [FFG+04], SOAP supports 'stateful' interactions. Within a stateful web service the service provider stores information about the client / consumer over a series of requests and is able to respond to these in coherence [Bir12 p.213] and [AG05 p.29]. Especially with increasing complexity of the web service this could be an advantage because the client does not need to set a state in each request. In other words: the client does not have to 'repeat' itself. On the contrary, this might also lead to an overhead for simple web services as many need- less states might be invoked and therefore also have to be considered by the interface designer.

As stated in [CDK+02] and **Figure 1: Structure of SOAP/WSDL** illustrated in Figure 1, SOAP can be used together with the Web Service Description Language (WSDL) to specify the meth- ods supported by the web service. It can be seen as a contract of communication between the client and the web service. WSDL explains the behavior of the interface formally with XML and hence is processable by machines. Therefore, with WSDL, client applications can discover and understand a web service easily. Due to the fact that interface designers try to make their web services easily adaptable and accessible for consumer applications, WSDL has become popular and is often used in coherence with SOAP.

Moreover, SOAP/WSDL can be extended with a lot of other specification standards which are informally called 'WS* Stack' [RR07, p. xv]. Referring to the large amount of modules and specifications in WS*, SOAP/WSDL and WS* are often called "big web services". The big variety and high quality of compatible extensions of WS* result in the advantage that additional specification modules can be integrated on demand, thus also web services with high feature demand are well supported by a SOAP-approach.

2.1.2 RESTful Web Services

As claimed by [RR07, pp. xv] and confirmed by Amazon[2] in the recent years RESTful web services have become a popular approach for the development of web based services.

In contrary to SOAP, a RESTful web service does not use further abstraction layers. Instead it is based on the RESTful Hyper Text Transfer Protocol (HTTP).

---

[2] Amazon is offering both SOAP and RESTful web services and consequently offers the opportunity to compare the popularity of both web service styles. A brief comparison can be found at [3].

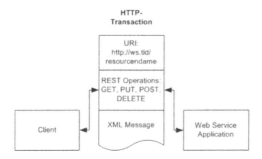

Figure 2: Structure of RESTful interaction

Figure 2 illustrates a RESTful web service interaction in accordance to [Fie00]: The concept of representational state transfer (REST) consists of three basic principles:

1. Identification of resources via URI ("nouns"). A resource is not necessarily a real-life entity, but could also be something more abstract such as "search". The main point is that URIs should be self-descriptive.
2. For all resources the same basic commands ("verbs") exist: GET, PUT, POST and DELETE.
3. Relationship and state transition is accomplished via hyperlinks and not by the server.

Because a RESTful web service basically uses the HTTP and does not require additional modules it is very light-weight. This also results in reduced complexity and very intuitive handling. Nevertheless, the dependence on the HTTP could also be seen as its major disadvantage because a RESTful web service cannot be adjusted to a new environment, e.g., different protocol.

As all the technologies which are involved (HTTP, XML) are very well established, the barriers for developers (of the service as well as of the client-applications) are very low. Due to the fact that the principles of HTTP are well known, the usage of such a web service is intuitive and the implementation very swift.

As stated in [PZL08] in spite of SOAP, RESTful services are stateless. This means that the service provider does not transit into a different state after a request. On the contrary: it always stays in a neutral default state. This leads to a reduction of complexity as the programmer does not have to consider follow-up states. Nevertheless, it is still possible to work statefully with

REST by using the URI to express different states. In other words: the RESTful service itself is stateless, but the client can invoke states by the choice of the URIs.

Anyway, due to the fact that URIs are used to identify the web service's resources, one major limitation can be observed: the length of the URI is restricted depending on the web server[3]. For small and simple web services this limitation will not be of significance, but if one considers more complex WS which require a lot of parameters, this restriction might become a big obstacle.

Thus, RESTful web services seem to be a good choice for simple and light-weight services.

2.1.3 Conclusion and Decision for RESTful Approach

Regarding the scope of the location validation web service, the decision for a RESTful implementation was made. This was based on a few particular reasons.

First of all, in general, SOAP is the better approach for complex web services, whereas REST works sufficient for simple services. Also current research papers such as [PZL08] recommend this decision-strategy:

> "The main conclusion from this comparison is to use RESTful services for tactical, ad hoc integration over the Web (à la Mashup) and to prefer WS-* Web services in professional enterprise application integration scenarios with a longer lifespan and advanced QoS requirements."

Considering that the location validation web service will basically consist of a single functionality, this clearly favors the RESTful approach. Furthermore, due to the fact that the web service will be running in the internet, the protocol restriction (to HTTP) of RESTful WS does not pose an obstacle for the project. A further point is the fact that location validation does not require any stateful interactions. All validation requests can be treated independently. In addition, there is a lack of current literature describing the implementation of RESTful services. Therefore, the choice for REST might contribute more value to the research community. Last but not least, one will not require any further modules of the WS* stack, and therefore do not have any dependence on SOAP.

---

[3] For example according to [4] the Apache standard configuration currently limits the requests to 8190 bytes.

2.1.4 Slim PHP Framework

Slim-PHP is a light-weight framework which can be used to implement RESTful web services in PHP. Firstly released in 2011, it has already gained wide popularity within the PHP-Community. It basically manages all REST-requests and delegates them.

The main reason to use a web service framework is that the implementation effort of the actual web services functionality will be reduced and an easy extensibility is guaranteed. Furthermore, this leaves more time to concentrate on core functionality.

The interested reader can find an introduction to Slim-PHP on the official web site [5].

2.2 GeoNames

GeoNames [6] is a free geographical database which consists of over 10 million geographical names. It is an important component of this project because it provides an interface to access the database with a variety of different methods. Especially the search function which can be used to find a location (and information about it) is of interest. The search function also supports a fuzzy-search which is very useful to correct misspellings. Furthermore all GeoNames search results are classified. Therefore it is possible to find out what kind of search result was found (e.g. City, State, Country).

A complete documentation of the GeoNames web service can be found online [7].

3   System Design

In the following the problem of the client applications will be described. Afterwards the resulting requirements for the validation web services will be detected.

3.1   Problem

A lot of applications process input data from users. Often also a geographical location is part of the input. In many cases, e.g., when the location information gets digitalized from paper, e.g., mail delivery, the application cannot ad-hoc work with this data and guarantee that the data is valid.

In this concrete scenario the client application manages a research conference database. The location-entries of the database are extracted out of full-text-emails. Consequently this scenario is very similar to the digitalization from paper as it can occur that the wrong part of the text has been recognized as location or that it contains (spelling) mistakes. Furthermore the client has no semantic information about the location string. This means, it cannot classify the parts of the string, e.g., which part of the string is a city, which is the country etc. Last but not least, depending on the spelling, also the consistence of the data is arguable, e.g., "Hawaii, U.S.A." vs. "Hawaii, United States" vs. "Hawaii, USA" vs. "Hawaii" (see Appendix 1).

3.2   Requirements and Structure

First of all, the validation web service will need to provide an interface for interaction with the clients. Thru this interface the full-text-location-strings will be transferred. It is necessary to process these according to the delimiters such as commas. Afterwards the application must assume an expected classification of each part of the location-string (city, country, state, etc.).

Then the application will need to verify its assumed location-data. To do so it will need to communicate with a geographical database, in particular GeoNames.

A critical part of the application is to draw the right assumptions out of the responses of GeoNames-request. E.g., if "Berlin" was assumed to be a Country, the GeoNames service will not be able to find it. The resulting major question is which conclusion the application will draw. Either it could assume that "Berlin" is still a Country and just misspelled or it might be the name of a City. One can see that a lot of different assumptions and combinations of these will be necessary to achieve a correct result. In the Section 4.2 this process will be illustrated.

After the communication with GeoNames is completed, the application has to respond to the client richly: the verified and unified response shall be classified by usage of XML and finally sent back to the client application.

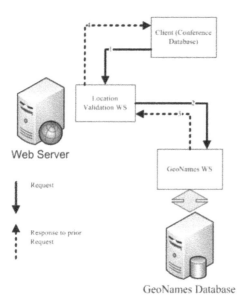

Figure 3: Chain of Interactions

Figure 3 illustrates the above described structure and the underlying communication process.

The interaction steps which are marked in Figure 3 can be explained as follows:

1. The conference database requests a location validation.
2. In order to fulfill the request from the conference database the location validation web service invokes a search in the GeoNames database.
3. GeoNames returns results. Depending on the progress step two might be repeated with different parameters.
4. The validation web service returns the final response to the conference database.

4   Implementation

The main validation functionality is encapsulated in a class LocationValidator-Class. For each validation request, which is received by the web service interface (Slim-PHP; Section 2.1.4) a new instance of the LocationValidator is created and executed. Finally the response of LocationValidator is extracted by calling the method createXMLResponse() and then returned to the client by the web interface.

Because the actual validation logic is encapsulated in the LocationValidator and detached from the web service interface, the code reusability is high.

In the following the main methods of the LocationValidor will be explained.

4.1   Splitting the string

In a first step the string of the request from the client is split into different parts by the locationSplit()-Function. In general, the delimiter is a comma, but also other delimiters can occur and are handled. Afterwards the different parts are classified and empty parts are dismissed.

In the sample data one could observe, that the geographical scope gets narrower from the right to the left. Consequently, the validator expects a city-name to be left of the country name etc. This "location-scope-theorem" is used to pre-classify the parts and supports the entire validation process.

The classification of the LocationValidator supports four different location-parts: Place, City, State and Country. A "place" is an unofficial geographical location (usually within a city), which cannot be found in the GeoNames database. Concrete examples for places are Universities and Hotels.

One special case in the sample data was observed: sometimes the location string passed from the client actually consists of more than one location, e.g., "Berlin + Hannover, Germany". In a naive approach this would lead to a validation error because "Berlin + Hannover" could not be found as a single city name in GeoNames. As a solution, in such a case the split-method treats all of these locations separately by creating new sub instances of itself for each of them and finally merging the result.

After the string parts have been extracted and temporary classified the actual validation is invoked.

4.2   Validating the Country

The validation of the country is critical to the success of the complete validation process, because an invalid country will prevent the narrowing of the geographical scope.

In some cases the expected country part proofs itself as a state. This usually happens when the state is very prominent and people therefore omit the country because to them it is self-explanatory. This problem is solved by generally requiring any administrative (states and countries) results from GeoNames which matches to the string part. Referring to the prior stated observations the following cases have to be considered.

Country is valid

If GeoNames returns a result of the type country, the validator can be sure that the last string part really is a country and already save it as a result-country. Afterwards the other parts of the string can be validated with regard to the narrowed geographical scope. This means that we will expect the result-city and state to be in that same country.

Valid State instead of Country

If GeoNames returns a result of the type state, the validator can save the last part as the result-state and furthermore derive the corresponding country and save it in the country-result. The validator then knows that the second last string part cannot be a state anymore (because a valid one (state) was found already) and therefore it has to be assumed that it is a city. All other parts of the string will be part of the street / place, which gets compressed into the place-result. According to our location-scope-rule we assume that the city will be most right part of the remainder.

Neither Country nor State is valid

If both prior cases do not work, we might assume that the string part is misspelled. Therefore a fuzzy-search in GeoNames will be invoked and then the prior steps will be repeated. If also this is without success, an error-response will be created as it proofed itself not possible to achieve a stable validation without having a state or country identified.

4.3 Validating other Parts

The validation of the other parts of the string is done analog to the country-validation. This means, that an invalid state will be checked if this could be a city etc.

The last location part might be a place such as a hotel or university building. Because such places in general are not listed in GeoNames, the place cannot be validated.

4.4   Accessing GeoNames

The building and execution of request to GeoNames is capsuled in the geoNamesRequest()-Method.

To access GeoNames the client URL Library was used (cURL) [8]. cURL can be used in the context of PHP to access a remote URL and retrieve its response. It is of great importance to set the right parameters whilst using cURL: CURLOPT_RETURNTRANSFER must be set true.

The geoNamesRequest-Method parses the XML-Response of the cURL-Request as a Simple-XML-Object [9] and therefore makes it very easily accessible within the application.

4.5   Test-Application

To assure the quality of the validation a test-script was necessary. It reads all the sample locations from a file (each line is expected to be one location string) and then accesses the validation web service in order to validate them. The input-location string and the response are then outputted in a table. Furthermore, the script counts all successful validations and error responses.

5   Testing

In order to evaluate the quality of the location validation web service the prior introduced test script was run with 500 sample location strings. In doing so a validation rate of 96% could be achieved. Afterwards it was evaluated if all valid-marked locations really were correctly validated and all invalid locations were legally declared invalid by the web service.

H0: Location is valid		
	H0 is true	H0 is false
Validator rejects H0	Type I error: 7	13
Validator does not reject H0	480 (96%)	Type II error: 0

Table 1: Test Results

Table 1 contains the detailed result of the validation. It was discovered that none of the validated strings were validated unjustified. This means that the Type II error in the sample data has been observed as 0%. In contrast, of all not validated location strings (the 4%) a 35% Type I error could be observed.

6   Conclusion and Outlook

This last Section summarizes the results of the project. Finally, improvement opportunities and research topics for further projects are proposed.

To my mind, the implementation of the LocationValidator forms a good base and can easily be extended to suite different needs. As shown in the Section 5 the implementation leads to a high validation rate. Due to the fact that the Type II Error is very low (0%), one can be certain that a location string which was validated successfully really is valid. On the other hand, the Type I Error is fairly high (35% of 4%) and therefore location strings which were declared as invalid by the LocationValidtor should be checked by a human being before a final rejection is triggered.

Whilst developing the application, it was observed that the reduction of the Type I Error usually results in a higher Type II error and contra wise. As the effort to control rejected validations in the 4% is a lot smaller than to find an unjustified validated location in the 96%, it was chosen to minimize the Type II error. Certainly, one could also reduce the amount of Type I Errors even more, but this would lead to a disproportionally high increase of effort because a lot more special cases would have to be considered. This optimization could be topic of another project.

All in all, I believe that the current implementation has a good cost-benefit ratio considering the achieved results in relation to the necessary implementation effort.

Within the project a few opportunities could be discovered which will be outlined in the following.

First of all, a general problem is that GeoNames does not sort its results by probability. For example a search request for "Utah" will return a place in Papua New Guinea instead of the state in the U.S.A, although naturally the likelihood that the requestor means the place in the U.S.A is a lot higher. This problem cannot be solved by the location validation service but by the provider of the geographical database.

Secondly, in line with the first point it would be of interest to alter the geographical database used by the LocationValidator. Especially an implementation which uses the Google Maps database could lead to an interesting comparison. At a first glance on the API documentation [10] the Google Maps API seems to provide a powerful full-text address validation method.

Last but not least, the conference database features could be easily extended. A first idea would be to provide a map which contains markers at the places of the conferences. Each marker could be connected with the corresponding conference dataset. Also features like a country-filter could be implemented.

References

[CDK+02]   Francisco Curbera, Matthew Duftler, Rania Khalaf,William Nagy, Nirmal Mukhi, Sanjiva Weerawarana. *Unraveling the Web Services Web: An Introduction to SOAP,WSDL, and UDDI*. IEEE, April 2002.

[LLS06]   Kenneth C. Laudon, Jane P. Laudon, Detlef Schoder. *Wirtschaftsinformatik: Eine Einführung*. Pearson, 2006.

[Alo04]   Gustavo Alonso. *Web Services: Concepts, Architectures and Applications*. Springer, 2004.

[AG05]   Akhil Sahai, Sven Graupner. *Web Services In The Enterprise: Concepts, Standards, Solutions, And Management*. Springer, 2005.

[Bir12]   Kenneth P. Birman. *Guide to Reliable Distributed Systems: Building High-Assurance Applications and Cloud-Hosted Services*. Springer, 2012.

[Fie00]   Roy T. Fielding. *Architectural Styles and the Design of Network-based Software Architectures*. PhD thesis, University of California, Irvine, 2000

[FGA+04]   Christopher Ferris, Sharad Garg, Daniel Austin, Abbie Barbir. Web services architecture requirements, February 2004.

[GCD05]   Tim Kindberg George Coulouris, Jean Dollimore. *Distributed Systems: Concepts and Design*. Addison Wesley, 2005.

[FFG+04]   Ian Foster, Jeffrey Frey, Steve Graham: Modeling Stateful Resources with Web Services. Whitepaper, 2004.

[RR07]   Leonard Richardson, Sam Ruby. *Restful Web Services*. O'Reilly,2007.

[PZL08]   Cesare Pautasso, Olaf Zimmermann, Frank Leymann. *RESTful Web Services vs. "Big" Web Services: Making the Right Architectural Decision*. WWW 2008, April 21–25, 2008, Beijing, China

Web Resources

[1]   http://www.w3.org/TR/ws-gloss/
[2]   http://www.w3.org/TR/soap/
[3]   http://www.oreillynet.com/pub/wlg/3005
[4]   http://httpd.apache.org/docs/2.2/mod/core.html#limitrequestline
[5]   http://www.slimframework.com/learn
[6]   http://www.geonames.org
[7]   http://www.geonames.org/export/web-services.html
[8]   http://www.php.net/manual/en/book.curl.php
[9]   http://de2.php.net/manual/en/book.simplexml.php
[10]   https://developers.google.com/maps/documentation/geocoding/

Appendix

1) Inconsistence in conference database

		Documents		
Jan 5th, 2004	Jan 8th, 2004	HICSS Minitrack on Enterprise Content Management and XML	Hawaii, USA	Mar 31st, 2003
Jan 5th, 2004	Jan 8th, 2004	HICSS-37 Minitrack on Mobile Distributed Information Systems	Hawaii, USA	Apr 10th, 2003
Jan 5th, 2004	Jan 8th, 2004	HICSS Minitrack on Distributed Object and Component-Based Software Systems	Waikoloa, Hawaii, USA	Mar 31st, 2003
Jan 5th, 2004	Jan 8th, 2004	HICSS Minitrack on Methods, Tools and Applications for Web-Based Integration of Financial and Logistic Supply Chains	Hawaii, United States	Mar 31st, 2003
Jan 5th, 2004	Jan 8th, 2004	HICSS Minitrack on Mobile Commerce: Core Business Technology and Intelligent Support	Waikoloa Village, Big Island, Hawaii, USA	Mar 31st, 2003
Jan 6th, 2004	Jan 9th, 2004	HICSS Minitrack Cluster on Information Technology and Public Administration	Big Island, Hawaii, Hawaii	Jun 1st, 2003
Jan 3rd, 2005	Jan 6th, 2005	The Semantic Web: The Goal of Web Intelligence (HICSS 2005)	Waikoloa, Hawaii, USA	Mar 31st, 2004
Jan 3rd, 2005	Jan 6th, 2005	HICSS Minitrack on Distributed Object and Component-Based Software Systems	Waikoloa, Hawaii, USA	Jun 15th, 2004
Jan 3rd, 2005	Jan 6th, 2005	Adaptive and Evolvable Software Systems: Techniques, Tools, and Applications (HICSS-AESS)	Big Island, Hawaii, USA	Jun 15th, 2004
Jan 3rd, 2005	Jan 6th, 2005	Fault-Tolerant and Dependable Distributed Systems (HICCS FTDDS)	Hilton Waikoloa Village, Big Island, Hawaii, U.S.A.	Jun 15th, 2004
Mar 12th, 2005	Mar 12th, 2005	2nd Workshop on Context Modeling and Reasoning (COMOREA)	Kauai Island, Hawaii, USA	Oct 1st, 2004
Jun 13th, 2005	Jun 16th, 2005	Symposium on Wireless IP (Part of WirelessCom 2005)	Sheraton Maui Resort, Kaanapali Beach, Maui, Hawaii, USA	Mar 15th, 2005
Oct 10th, 2005	Oct 10th, 2005	Special Session at IEEE SMC 2005 Ensemble Methods for Extreme Environments	Waikoloa, Hawaii, USA	Mar 1st, 2005
Nov 9th, 2005	Nov 11th, 2005	18th International Conference on Computer Applications in Industry and Engineering (CAINE-2005)	Honolulu, Hawaii, USA	Jul 22nd, 2005
Jan 4th, 2006	Jan 7th, 2006	HICSS-39 Decision Technologies for Management Track	KAUAI, Hawaii, USA	Jun 15th, 2005
Jan 4th, 2006	Jan 7th, 2006	HICSS-39 Mini-Track: Contract Management and Decisions Support in Services Science	Kauai, Hawaii, USA	Jun 15th, 2005
Sep 16th, 2006	Sep 18th, 2006	The 2006 IEEE International Conference on Information Reuse and Integration (IEEE IRI-2006)	Waikoloa, Hawaii, USA	May 19th, 2006
Jan 3rd, 2007	Jan 6th, 2007	Visual Interactions in Software Artifacts (HICSS-40 Mini-track VISA'07)	Big Island, Hawaii, USA	Jun 15th, 2006
Jan 3rd, 2007	Jan 6th, 2007	Minitrack Tools for Model Driven Development at HICSS 40 (MDD)	Hawaii, USA	Jun 15th, 2006
Jan 3rd, 2007	Jan 6th, 2007	Recommender Systems (HICSS MiniTrack)	Waikoloa, Hawaii	Jun 15th, 2006
Apr 1st, 2007	Apr 5th, 2007	Special Session on Web Intelligence and Web Mining (WIWM)	Honolulu, Hawaii, USA	Nov 15th, 2006
Aug 13th, 2007	Aug 16th, 2007	16th International Conference on Computer Communications and Networks (ICCCN)	Honolulu, Hawaii, USA	Mar 18th, 2007

Four different spellings for U.S.A can be observed.